The
How to *easily* ∧
Handle
Difficult
People
Handbook

Everything Problem-People Don't Want You to Know

MURRAY OXMAN

SOURCEBOOKS, INC.®
NAPERVILLE, ILLINOIS

Published by Sourcebooks, Inc.
P.O. Box 4410, Naperville, Illinois 60567–4410
(630) 961–3900
FAX: (630) 961–2168
www.sourcebooks.com

Originally published in 1997

Library of Congress Cataloging-in-Publication Data
Oxman, Murray.
  The how to easily handle difficult people handbook : everything problempeople don't want you to know / Murray Oxman.
      p. cm.
  Originally published: United States : Success Without Stress, 1997.
  ISBN-13: 978-1-4022-0694-8
  ISBN-10: 1-4022-0694-1
 1. Interpersonal conflict. 2. Interpersonal communication. I. Title.

BF637.I48O96 2006
158.2--dc22

                                                        2006008205

          Printed and bound in the United States of America.
                LB 10 9 8 7 6 5 4 3 2 1

This book is dedicated to the memory of
Vernon Howard with the utmost respect
and gratitude.

Preface:
About This Book

Upon first reading this guidebook we were amazed. It's more correct to say we were really shocked—but in a good way. It woke us up to how much we didn't know about the psychology of being human. We sensed deeply that this was no ordinary book. The answers all rang true!

We went to the author, Murray Oxman, and asked how he had arrived at such a departure from what we call normal psychology. Murray replied that three things had greatly influenced him. First, everything he had previously tried didn't work.

Second, he resorted to the Golden Rule— "Do unto others as you would have them do unto you."

And last, but not least, in his search for self-understanding, he met a man who always treated him correctly. He said it was from this man's actions—from his being—that he learned all he wanted to know. Murray laughed when he added, "I learned the most from the things I didn't want to know!" He then said, "The man was a famous author, speaker, and teacher. I have my own reasons for not revealing his name. Very few people would pay the price to be around him and learn from him. The price one had to pay was to allow him to show you what you are really like as opposed to the phony act you present to everyone. One's egotism was constantly being bruised. Thank God this man was sent from Above to help any and all who wanted true help. Most people preferred not to get close to him. They simply read his books and attended his talks."

Murray went on to say this book is not about gaining an ego victory over another person but about treating people rightly. He added that when you treat people rightly you are truly being good to them. However, you can never treat anyone correctly if you want something from them. He continued by saying he was very grateful for those in his life who didn't put up with his nonsense and wished everyone would

have treated him early on in his life as he out-
lines in this guidebook. Murray feels it would
have made him look at himself quite differently—which would have been very healthy
and helpful. He concluded by saying, "If we all
treated one another rightly—with no malice—
think what a better world this could be."

After listening to what Murray had to say
and rereading this handbook, we came to the
conclusion that we unknowingly had been
sabotaging our own lives—and we're grateful
for the insight. Now we don't have to do it
anymore.

—The Publishing Team

Introduction

Once upon a time long ago and far away there lived a small group of people in a village at the edge of a vast and beautiful forest. The men of the village planted and hunted while the women gathered all kinds of delicious foods in the nearby forest.

One day while in the forest picking flowers for their hair, the ladies were frightened by a big tiger. When the men heard about what happened, they ran into the forest to drive the tiger away. When the men found the tiger, they took one look at it, turned on their heels, and fled. It was the biggest, fiercest looking tiger they had ever seen.

Back in the village the men and women met to decide what to do about the tiger. They felt helpless and scared. Then one man suggested, "Let's go ask the Old Wise Man of our village what we should do." They all agreed this was a good idea.

The sun was high in the sky and all eyes were on the Old Wise Man as he walked calmly, staff in hand, into the forest. It was more than two hours before he was seen returning from the forest. Everyone sighed a sigh of relief. They had been concerned that maybe the worst had happened to the Old Wise Man. When he was close enough so all could hear, he asked them to meet with him at sundown in front of his home. They all agreed to be there.

The sun was setting as all the villagers gathered to hear what the Old Wise Man had to tell them. He stood before them, looking them over, making eye contact first with one and then with another. Then a warm smile appeared on his face as he announced, "You will not be bothered by the tiger again. He's gone."

Someone asked, "How did you do it?"

"How did I do it? Well, this is how: first I must tell you I have always been fond of observing tigers. In my youth I spent many hours in the forest hoping to see a tiger. Whenever I found one I would keep my distance and just watch. Many tigers in the forest came to know me by sight and scent and allowed me to observe them.

"Today when I came upon your tiger it did not take me long to understand what was going on here. When you know tigers as I do you can easily spot anything out of the ordinary—which I did quickly. Your tiger did not act like any tiger I had ever seen. It aroused my suspicions, so I decided to observe it at a distance. The more I watched, the more my suspicions were confirmed. So I stepped out of my hiding place and walked straight towards the tiger."

At this point an anxious murmur rippled through the villagers. The Old Wise Man continued, "It turns out your tiger was a fake tiger. Some mischievous boys from the neighboring village had taken a tiger skin they had found and draped it over their bodies to scare people in the forest. When they realized I was not frightened and was onto them, they soon took off their disguise and confessed. I scolded them and made them promise to return the tiger skin to where it belonged and not to ever frighten people again. I feel certain that's the end of the problem."

This story is a perfect illustration for understanding difficult people. They're all, in reality, undisciplined children wearing a disguise.

This guidebook will show you how to understand them and see through the masks they're wearing. Any difficult person can be handled with complete ease, confidence, and poise.

Our lofty aim is to learn all about human nature while not being critical of people. You're not being critical when you say someone is a difficult person if that's a fact and you don't resent them. When we better understand others, we better understand ourselves.

The Twenty Most Difficult People

The following is a list of the nineteen most well-known types of difficult people and a mysterious twentieth type—The Most Difficult Person of All. Keep in mind, some difficult people fall into more than one category.

1. The Gloom and Doomer
2. The Intimidator
3. The Energy Thief
4. Mr. Obnoxious
5. The Criticizer
6. The Judge
7. The Trash Man
8. The Persister
9. The Moaner and Groaner
10. The Moocher
11. The Demander

This handbook is designed so you may look through the above list and then turn to the numbers that most interest you. Or you might like to just leaf through the pages of difficult people at random. They're in no particular order. For the sake of convenience this guide is written using the male gender. (Of course women can sometimes be difficult people, too.)

Each type of difficult person is described and an appropriate response suggested. Sometimes examples will be given. Some responses might make you feel a little uncomfortable at first. Don't be deterred. Just remember that your old responses didn't work or you wouldn't be reading this. A nice thing about the new responses is that you will do them consciously because they are different. You'll be consciously uncomfortable. Good!

Here's something you can observe for yourself: because difficult people are mechanical in their actions they need certain responses from you to continue their bad behavior. When they no longer get the response they seek, they have no choice but to look elsewhere.

Check it out!

1

The Gloom and Doomer

Description: This person loves to say anything that spreads fear and depression. He actually gets a thrill out of watching his victim feel bad. (Does our news media fall into this category?)

Response: First, as the person is speaking, say silently to yourself, "This time he has the wrong person." Then, when you can get a word in edgewise into the conversation—you may have to interrupt the person—say, "Excuse me, I have something important I need to do right now," and walk away. Of course the important thing you need to do you've done. You sent a strong message that says, "I'll not allow myself to be dragged down to your level."

The Intimidator

Description: There are many ways people bully and intimidate. Some use anger, negativity, or a mean expression on their face; others use a certain tone of voice. In addition, a person's general manner can be intimidating.

Response: Know that this person is a frightened person. He or she carefully studies your reactions and uses them against you. Not everyone is intimidated by the same bully. Change your reactions and you'll be rid of the bully. Never fawn before anyone, especially a bully. A weak smile on your face attracts an attack. Expressing any kind of negativity toward the person adds fuel to the fire. That's exactly what he wants.

Simply look right at the person, even if you are shaking inside, with a look of disbelief on your face. You can't believe an adult would act so childish. Your facial expression lets the person know you will not be frightened by bad manners.

Afterwards you'll realize a very beautiful fact. You called the bluff on two bullies. The first being the difficult person we're discussing, and the second being the one trembling inside you.

Example: This is one of the most powerful guides revealed in this handbook: you don't have to answer a question just because it is asked! It is quite common for intimidating people to ask all kinds of wrong questions about your personal life. Maybe they'll ask about your financial affairs or something else of a private nature that really has nothing at all to do with the subject you're discussing.

The next time this happens give them a jolt by saying, "Why are you asking me that question?" Then, while they're reeling from the jolt, follow up with, "Let's keep this conversation on the subject at hand." In doing this you've correctly taken charge of the conversation. Afterwards reflect on what happened, not for ego gratification, but to better understand how the dynamics of the law of cause and effect work in human relations.

3

The Energy Thief

Description: Have you ever felt so drained after a conversation with someone you weren't sure you'd make it through the rest of the day? You just had a conversation with a thief—an energy thief. Personal energy is very important. The energy thief wastes his, and now he wants to steal yours. He loves to hear the sound of his own voice, so he talks, talks, and talks some more. He loves to say negative things. He also loves to gossip and do anything to draw you into a conversation and/or into his negativity—which is highly contagious and unhealthy!

That's right, being negative harms your body and your spirit! Of course he never considers you may have better things to do than let him drain your energy. His aim is to harm you as he's hurt himself.

Response: The best thing you can do is not to get into a conversation with the person in the first place. He has no conscience! Be alert. If possible, when you see him coming your way, leave. If you can't leave, just nod your head every minute or two and say, "I understand." You're not agreeing with him, but just simply acknowledging you hear him (and you understand what he's up to). If he asks questions, make your replies as short as possible. Answer yes or no and nothing more when appropriate. In some cases, you may want to ignore him completely when he speaks to you. Stay very alert. Do not get drawn into a conversation—that's what he wants.

Remember he isn't at all interested in anything but stealing your energy. Sometime, if possible, observe him in a conversation with another person. Notice he never really listens to the other person because he isn't interested in what they're saying. He's just waiting for any opportunity to speak again himself.

Unnecessary talking is a tremendous waste of energy. See if you don't feel a lot better at the end of the day when you don't overdo the talking.

Mr. Obnoxious

Description: This is the person who's starved for attention. That's right. He does all of those ill-mannered things to shock you into noticing him. He wants to feel special and the only way he knows how is to be especially rude.

Response: Since he feeds on your attention, especially shocked attention, simply ignore his bad behavior. If he continues, walk away—but remember, he probably will fire a parting volley at you as you leave. Ignore it also.

Example: Someone tells an off-color joke. Don't laugh. This encourages the bad behavior when you go along with it. If others are present and they laugh, you need to be the strong one who doesn't! Most people laugh out of nervousness, not because they think the joke is funny.

The Criticizer

Description: The news media are the perfect example. The Criticizer is someone who is very critical of everything and everyone but himself.

Response: The one thing that always defuses this kind of problem-person is to simply agree with him when he criticizes you. Before you start to argue with this, please try it! See if you don't immediately feel an amazing inner-freedom. Try saying something like this to the person criticizing you: "You know, you might have something there—I'll look into it."

Example: Balzac, the famous French writer and mystic, was constantly and unjustly attacked by the critics of his day. When his friends asked him how he felt about it, he would reply, "Why should I let it bother me?—besides, they actually help me at times by pointing out ways to improve my art." His bright attitude was his personal light.

6

The Judge

Description: A judgmental person is always offering his supreme (in his eyes) opinion on just about everything. The fact that you did not ask for his opinion in the first place does not deter him at all.

Response: When the judge will allow it, quietly make the following comment: "I promised myself that whenever I heard anyone judging another person, I would use it to remind me to adhere to the old adage: 'Never judge anyone until you've walked a mile in their shoes.' I am also to be reminded of something said by a very wise man. He suggested we always weigh what we say by these three nice guides: 'Is it true? Is it kind? Is it necessary?'"

You can feel assured the judge will get the message and hopefully be reminded of what Christ said, "Judge not lest ye be judged."

The Trash Man

Description: This is the person who wants you to clean up his trash—his problems. He wants to dump his trash on you! Why does he want you to help him? The answer is simple: he wants to avoid responsibility for his own life. Plus, if he can get you to give him advice, he has someone to blame if things don't turn out the way he wants.

You always hurt someone when you do anything that encourages him to not take full responsibility for his own life—including his mistakes and decisions.

Response: Use these very practical words that work like magic: "I decided long ago that one of the nicest things I could do for my friends was to not bore them with my problems and to not listen to theirs."

The Persister

Description: Have you ever had an evening meal interrupted by a phone call from a salesperson who wouldn't take "No" for an answer? When you said, "Thanks, but I'm not interested," he said, "Would you please tell me why?" You wanted to hang up but felt it would be rude, so you burned inwardly with resentment and continued the conversation. Maybe you even bought what he was selling, something you really didn't want, out of guilt over feeling resentful.

Response: After you have once said "No" and the person persists with his sales pitch and tricks—hang up. You are not being rude. He is. Don't feel guilty. His presentation is carefully scripted and depends on you wrongly feeling rude or guilty.

Example: Here's a similar situation with a little different twist: Someone asks you for something you do not want to give. Simply say "No." He then asks you to explain your answer. Now you reply sternly, "Because I don't want to." The person persists by asking again, "But why, please, can't you just tell me why?" Your reply is again stern, "You're wasting your time."

The Moaner and Groaner

Description: The moan and groan act can easily be recognized—the person always injects a little or a lot of moaning and/or groaning into whatever he says. Everything about him says, "Please feel sorry for me"—the way he talks, his posture, especially the expression on his face. This is to make sure you know he's carrying a heavy, heavy load. And of course his load, in his mind, is more than any human could possibly bear. So he moans and groans hoping you'll ask what the problem might be. And if you should, his reply of course would be, "You're so intuitive!—How did you know anything was going on with me?" (with a moan in his voice).

Response: If you ever make the mistake of asking what the problem might be, you're in for quite an earful—don't do it! Simply ignore the moaning and groaning. Don't take the bait. You'll have a much nicer day for it. It's important to remember that it hurts people to go along with their self-pity. And conversely it helps them when you don't—it snaps them out of it a bit. Wallowing in self-pity hurts us all.

The Moocher

Description: This is the type who always wants something for nothing. People in advertising know the strongest word in any ad is FREE! Everyone wants something for nothing. And yet, nothing feels better than achieving something through hard work. There's a right part in all of us that likes us to earn our own way. We all know there really are no free lunches.

Response: When you give anyone an unearned benefit you hurt him. You strip him of his human dignity. That doesn't mean you might not want to give a hungry man a meal, but we all know the difference between a man down on his luck and a man who has discovered how to get by without earning his own way. Have you noticed that the more "help" there is available, the more people there are to take advantage of the "help"? Most people will agree—in this country anybody who really wants to work can find a job.

The same holds true for young people in your family—the nicest thing you can do is to encourage them to be self-reliant.

The Demander

Description: "You owe me. I was there when you needed me, now I need you. You owe me." Sound familiar? Isn't it strange we think of ourselves as kind, caring, giving people, but at the same time we feel you owe me for my kindness? The fact is we want to build up a credit balance for future use. We're trading. We're exploiting one another. That is neither nice nor kind.

Response: Never play trading games with people. If you really want to do something for someone, do it! No strings attached. If you don't—don't! No one owes you, and you owe no one. Clear cut, pure, and nice!

Touchy Touchy

Description: Someone once aptly compared being around people like this to walking on eggshells. They're overly sensitive. And they love to feel offended.

Response: Being around this kind of person is like having your own gold mine. There are rich rewards to be had. Here's why: There's no such thing as a difficult person. Sure, some people are very troublesome. But these people can also be very useful. Here's how: The real problem is not other people but our own inner reaction to them. If any given difficult person was truly the problem, everyone would see this person as difficult, but they don't.

To repeat, the real problem is in us. And that's good news! Why? You can't change another person. We've all tried and failed many, many times. But here's something that always works! We can change our reactions to people. We can let go of the negative reaction inside us. When we let go of this negative reaction we're instantly free of the difficult person. Sounds nice, doesn't it? It is!

You're probably thinking something like, "Yes, it sounds great, but how do I do it?" The answer is so simple it has been overlooked by everyone except a few dedicated people who sincerely wanted Real Life more than pain and suffering. The answer is: Do Nothing! That's right, do nothing!

Example: You're with a touchy person. You say or do something that bothers him. He reacts by saying something negative to you or by sulking. Now you have a negative reaction like you've had so often in the past, but this time you do something new and different. You simply observe your negativity, you stand aside and watch it. It wants you to say or do something in response to the man's negative behavior.

You watch this go on inside you and you do nothing about it. You refuse to express the negativity. And like magic, neither the difficult person nor the negativity in you has any power over you. Your newfound understanding has set you free. This is what Christ taught: "Turn the other cheek"—which is so misunderstood.

The Know-It-All

Description: This person knows everything about everything—so he believes. If you have the unfortunate experience of having a conversation with this type of difficult person, you will immediately recognize him. No matter what you say, his reply is always, "I know, I know."

Response: If you are attempting to explain something, even of great practical importance, to this kind of person, often there is no choice but to drop the subject for a while. Often if you take it up again at a different time the person will be more receptive. Use this as an opportunity to observe how people can change personalities from moment-to-moment, day-to-day.

Here's another tack that often works: After the person has given you a few, "I know, I know" responses, say something like this:

"There are parts of what we are discussing that I don't fully understand. Please tell me all you know."

Mr. Bossy

Description: Have you encountered people who are bossy, critical, and generally hard to get along with? That's Mr. Bossy himself. There are definite reasons a person acts this way. Inwardly they are scared and very unhappy. Their fear and unhappiness is hidden from them by their unpleasant behavior toward people. It makes them feel unnaturally better by being contrary and bossy.

Response: Be very alert when dealing with Mr. Bossy. Most of us react in one of two ways. We either react in a subservient way, or we get our dander up and get negative. Neither is correct. And what's more, if we simply watch our reactions and refuse to react to them negatively, there's no problem handling this kind of person. One just calmly and matter-of-factly goes about the business at hand.

Note: When we get negative we are not reacting to something someone said or did. We are reacting negatively to our own negative reactions. Please become keenly interested in this, and study the whole process for yourself. Self-understanding is powerful.

Mr. Inward

Description: This person is the exaggerated introvert that is so turned inward that it is extremely difficult to communicate with him. Plus, he can be very unpleasant. He's swimming in a sea of self-harming thoughts and feelings. He never thinks of anything but himself.

Response: First, do not take this person's actions personally. Most of the time they have nothing to do with you. And even if they do— still, do not take them personally. This is a very frightened individual. Remember this is not about hurting people. It is about discovering the secrets of nice human relations. Sometimes it's correct to be firm. Other times we must be gentle. What works most often with this type of difficult person is a pleasant smile. It usually jolts the person out of himself a little. Remember your smile must never imply weakness. Scared people are weak people. And weak people will psychologically pounce other people they sense are weak. Your smile must suggest only friendliness.

Also, be patient. A healthy dose of patience never hurts anyone.

Example: You are at work and Mr. Inward approaches you and starts complaining about one of your products.

First, you do not want to do something to alienate a customer. Even if he is a pain to deal with. Second, that person is part of our school of life. We need to learn how to act rightly toward everyone.

Your first reaction is to feel negative about the customer. Don't do it! Instead put a genuine smile on your face to let the person know you want to resolve their problem for them. You think that would be phony—right? Please consider this: the negative feeling is the true phony here. Your true nature can't ever get negative.

If there is also a feeling of impatience inside you that says, "Just get rid of this person," ignore that feeling. Instead be patient and helpful. In most cases the person will respond kindly toward you. Try it for yourself.

The Blabber

Description: You go to a person that you hope is going to solve some problem you have. And you're paying for the visit. This person is supposed to be a professional. You never figured on the person giving you an earache by blabbing, blabbing, and blabbing about his life. What a shock! This is a very common type of difficult person.

Response: After you shake off the shock, say something like, "That's really interesting, let's discuss it sometime over lunch. But right now I'm most concerned with the problem at hand—mine. Can we please attend to that?"

Example: You go to a health professional for advice about a physical problem you're having. The person asks you some questions and discusses the problem a bit. Then the next thing you know, he's telling you all about his life and problems. Stop it early on. Remember you're paying your hard earned money for the visit. If the person slips back into this rude behavior again don't hesitate to remind him again, "I'm paying you for this time, please stick to my problem."

Note: Make it a habit to notice how often total strangers will, given the opportunity, indiscreetly tell you their life story.

17

The Activist

Description: This person is on a mission. He feels that he has been personally chosen to change the world. He feels that he is pure as new fallen snow and is not part of the world's problems. And he always knows how to solve mankind's woes, and insists on telling you all he knows. The problem is that he wants to change everything but himself.

Response: "Sir, I mean no disrespect, but it has been my experience that like charity, change must start at home. Changing the masses for the better will not happen. But you and I can change. We can refuse to harbor anything inside of us that is not decent and nice. If we do that, it will change the world."

The Excuse Machine

Description: The Excuse Machine has an excuse for every time he makes a mistake or does not follow through on a task he was assigned to do. "I made a mistake," or "I was wrong," are sentences that he has never used. The sad thing about this kind of person is, if he would use his brain for right thinking and learn from his mistakes, instead of making worn out excuses, he'd surely do better at whatever he's doing.

Response: Of course each encounter with a difficult person is different so one must always respond somewhat differently depending on circumstances. Above all else, do not be mean-spirited when you respond. Be firm. This is a general way to respond: "My dear fellow, if you want to go through life excusing your irresponsibility, that's your business. But the fact is, you did not do what you said you'd do. I have things to do, and I do not have time to play games.

"One more thing—do yourself a real favor and read *A Message to Garcia*. It's a great short story by Elbert Hubbard. And read Rudyard Kipling's marvelous poem 'If.' Good day."

19

The Kibitzer

Description: Someone who butts into the affairs of others, sticks in his nose or "two-cents." Kibitzers tell others what they should do or not do, and yet their lives are generally awful. It's a case of "the pot calling the kettle black."

Response: Tell the Kibitzer that all of his suggestions are excellent and appreciated. But since he thought of them, he should pay any monies and do the work necessary to implement them.

Example: You have decided to homeschool your children. An acquaintance of yours is a classical Kibitzer. He continually brings up the subject of your children being homeschooled. He says he is worried that they will miss all the interaction and socialization that goes on in schools. He thinks the children will be unable to cope in social situations when they are adults. The fact is he really knows nothing about the children's activities and time spent in social situations. He is just a classical Kibitzer.

After trying to explain to the person on several occasions that the children are developing socially quite well, you decide to have a little fun. Here's how: You call the Kibitzer on the phone and say that you want to get together for a bite to eat and some conversation. He agrees and you settle on having lunch the next day.

The next day at lunch, as you're eating, you say, "I've been thinking over all you have been saying about the possible negative consequences homeschooling can have on our children. The main reason we chose to homeschool the children is, we did not want them going to public school. We heard too many appalling reports. So I've done a lot of research and I have discovered a highly respected private school that we feel might be right for the children."

The Kibitzer replies, "I am so glad you have reconsidered. I'm sure it will be the right thing for your children."

Now you say: "Then we agree. By the way

the tuition is about $3,000 a year for each child. And since we can't afford it, we thought you would want to pay the tuition for us."

At this point you will most likely have one less difficult person in your life.

20

The Most Difficult Person of All

Description: This person rarely, if ever, admits he's wrong. He's sure he understands himself, others, and life. And yet his deep-seated unhappiness proves otherwise. Others see him as he actually is, but he can't honestly see himself. In his heart-of-hearts he knows this description fits him—but he also wants to ignore it. Who is this mystery person? It's none other than ourself. That's right, there's no more problematic person in our life than ourself. The truth of the matter is: no one causes our inner reactions but us. We suffer from our own inner reactions—not from other people's actions! Sure some people's behavior is inexcusable. But for us to hurt ourselves is also inexcusable—especially when we cannot do it anytime we choose! There is no right time to suffer psychologically over anything—period!

Response: Notice your reactions as they are happening. Stand aside as an interested observer. Don't judge what you see—just observe. You will discover a marvelous secret: the source of the pain is your own wrong reaction. "That person shouldn't do that!" The fact is they did do that—but you should not react as you do and it hurts you!

Example: Recently there was an article in the newspaper about a famous singer/actress. She said that when she was a child, her famous singer/actress mother was going through something in her life and when a friend said to her mother, "Just snap out of it!" she wanted to hit her mother's friend. She continued to say that years later when she, the daughter, was going through something and a friend said to her, "Just snap out of it!" she wanted to hit him and did. What a shame!

Unknowingly she was actually fighting for her sick right to hurt herself. In both cases the friends were giving healthy, sound advice. Yes, as an outsider it's much easier to see things clearly. But the fact remains we love to feel sorry for ourselves, we love to suffer—needlessly! And when someone says, "Just snap out of it!" we want to lash out at them. We must give up our childish behavior and grow up.

Please ponder this: it seems we have become a country of whiners—people who don't want to take responsibility for our own actions and lives. We always have an excuse for our bad behavior and shortcomings. The Founding Fathers of this country are surely turning over in their graves—whining was just not their style.

We must change our nature and change it now! True life is reserved for the spiritually mature.

The only real freedom that exists is inner freedom—freedom from our own hurtful reactions. The very recognition of the problem as the problem will start the healthy healing—and what a beautiful healing it is! Want that more than your present reactions and you can have it!

Helpful Questions and Answers from a Class Discussion in Corvallis, Oregon

1.

Is it possible to enter into any situation with any person and not be bothered or upset? Not be negative and blame others for how we feel?

The way we feel and the kind of life we have is our own responsibility. That's what it really amounts to. So, consequently, just think about it—there would be no difficult people at all if everybody approached life that way. But they don't. But you and I can; therefore, we're not going to be difficult people. And we're going to see through other people as well as ourselves. Consequently, because we've dissolved our reactions to them by not believing in the reactions, no one will be a difficult person for us anymore. You can do it!

2.

It seems to me that practically everyone I meet is a difficult person. Is that so, or is it just my point of view?

Everybody is a difficult person if you react incorrectly toward them. Nobody is a difficult person if you don't react incorrectly toward them.

3.

You list twenty difficult people. Is it true that I am like all of those people, but at different times?

Yes. I got these twenty people from observing myself. Anybody who's honest will admit that at one time or another they have been all of them. I certainly have.

4.

One of the difficult people is a bully—the Intimidator, I think. Are you saying there are two bullies: the person I am dealing with and the person inside of me?

Right. The bully appears to us to be a person. But that's not the way it really is. The real bully is your reaction to the person that you call a bully. The way you know a person is bullying you is that you have these reactions pushing you around. And then you blame it on another person. Seeing the facts as the facts is the beginning of the end of the inward bullying.

5.

I have a difficult person in my life who is so overbearing. Whenever I'm around the person I change from being rather outgoing and assertive to being very weak and timid.

That's an experience most of us have had. As always, the answer lies within each one of us. If my reaction tells me that the other person is someone I can be assertive with, then I'm assertive. But if my reaction is to be frightened,

I become very passive and timid. In the first case my reaction is what it is because I feel somewhat superior. It's easy to be outgoing and confident then. But if I get scared of someone, all of a sudden I don't feel superior. In fact, I feel just the opposite.

We can see then that, inside us, there is a duality. This duality is not part of who we really are. It was never intended for human beings to have that duality. And by working on yourself with the principles outlined in this book, a person can be made One. For instance, when a person is in a situation that makes him uncomfortable, he thinks there is himself *and* the uncomfortableness. He thinks these are two distinctly separate things. Factually, that is a trick of a divided mind—there is really only the uncomfortableness. There is no such thing as a separate self. If one does not try to get rid of the uncomfortableness, does not resist it, but just consciously observes it, the duality vanishes. Now you don't have the duality, the split. At that point you are neither the timid nor the assertive person. You're natural, not separate from anything, but One with everything. Please, don't think about it—feel it!

6.

One of my family members is very difficult. I can't say anything without him taking it wrong. How should I handle this?

You know what they say, "You can choose your friends, but you can't choose your family!" My best advice to you is get out of town! Seriously, I think we covered this in Touchy Touchy. What you never want to do is to respond negatively, as they want you to.

7.

At work if my boss talks to me in a certain tone of voice, no matter how hard I try not to, I cry. What should I do?

You're not in the onion slicing department are you? The problem is an inner problem. It has nothing to do with your boss. Just think about it. What a terrible way to go through life reacting to the tone of a person's voice or the look on their face. The real solution is to see that it really is an inner problem and go to work on it. But you must be perfectly clear in seeing it. You must see that it is a mechanical reaction. As a child, some

authority figure probably spoke to you in a particular way with a particular tone of voice. You most
likely had a negative reaction, which has stayed
with you all this time. This is conditioning. It can
only be dissolved by not reacting to the negative
reaction and just watching it and bearing the
uncomfortableness of it. This is one of those
things in life that can only be understood by doing
it. This is truly powerful, practical magic.

8.

**You mention Mr. Obnoxious in the book. A
certain person at work is always coming up
with really terrible remarks and jokes,
which I don't want to hear.**

In a situation where you can't get away from
such a person, you have to say, "Look! I'm not
interested in that. I'll be glad to talk to you about
something else, but those kind of things I don't
want to hear or talk about." It will give him and
you a little shock, but that's healthy. That's not
rude. The other person *is* rude, putting you in the
position where you have to handle it that way.

The inner and the outer are the same. If you
put up with any kind of negative reaction that

goes on inside of you, you'll put up with it outside you. I didn't say be a positive thinker. I'm
saying get rid of the negativity. Say to *yourself*,
"Knock it off! I'll have nothing to do with you!"
Otherwise negative people and reactions seek
you out because they know you are weak.

9.

**There's a Moocher in my life—always
asking me for money. How do I know when
it is the right thing and when it isn't?**

In general moochers are bums. Could it be that
the only reason I even consider giving them
what they want is because I have an image of
myself as being a kind, helpful person—a superior person? People who have that image of
themselves burn inwardly with resentment
because to uphold that image they do things
they really do not want to do.

You have to ask yourself this very simple
question: "Am I hurting this individual by
assuming some of his financial responsibility?" Sometimes you might be, sometimes
not. You have to ask that, and you have to
answer it.

10.

Where I work, everybody wants to dump their trash in my lap. They like to pour out all of their complaining or confusion. Are you saying I get trapped because I'm not vigilant?

Right. You aren't vigilant. You haven't learned your lesson. Could it be that you want people to think well of you? You want them to like you? There's no greater hell than wanting people to like you. Wanting people to like you makes you weak. Nobody likes a weak person. Don't be afraid of people not liking you.

11.

A person I work with can't do enough for me. We didn't get along at first, but now he's nothing but nice and helpful. What do you call this type of difficult person?

The Exploiter. He wants to get something from you, so he's giving you what he thinks you want so he can get what he wants. You tell people all kinds of things by your manner and behavior. He sees that he can exploit you, so he does. If we look honestly and clearly we can see that it all comes back to "me"—what am I doing to attract this to myself?

12.
Are The Judge and The Criticizer in the book really people who inhabit my own mind?

Right. If you are really astute and watch what goes on inside you, you will see that you are that way both with other people as well as with yourself. So you pay a big price for being that kind of person—for having that kind of nature. You have to change yourself, so that you no longer have that kind of nature. I didn't say to pretend that you're a different kind of person. I mean to really change—get rid of anything inside of you that is judgmental and criticizes. You can get rid of it anytime you want. Don't ask me how. Just do it. Look! You weren't born with it. You don't see little children judging and being critical. It's something that you did to yourself. So if you did it to yourself, you must undo it.

13.
You are often emphasizing self-responsibility. That's what we need?

Right! Just think about it! What would the world be like if everyone held themselves responsible for all their actions? I mean the inner-actions, too. You know, refusing to allow any negativity to take root and grow inside. The world would be unrecognizable to us. It is not going to happen. But you and I can make it happen for us. Then our inner-world will be Godly.

14.
It's an unpleasant experience to catch myself being one of the difficult people you describe in the book.

It's a marvelous experience, if you use it correctly! Self-knowledge is essential to spiritual growth. It's only uncomfortable to your ego, your false-self. You are not your ego, but you think you are. If you will just endure the unpleasantness and remain uncomfortable— that would be striking a blow for freedom from the egotism. You, like all of us, go through your life never being aware of what is going on inside of you. Most of the time you hide it from yourself. You do not want to know anything unsavory about yourself. But by being constantly aware of what's going on inside you, while not judging anything, and bearing the uncomfortableness, you invite the light of awareness to shine in and light up a formerly dark room. In that bright inner-room, you, from yourself, know who you really are: you are not the egotism! This is not new age mumbo jumbo. It is a fact.

15.
Why do I look at others and see that they are difficult, that they have lots of problems, but I don't see it in myself?

Comparison is a terrible thing. People usually do it to make themselves feel better or worse. But what kind of person would do that? Does someone with a sound mind and a sound spirit, need to compare? Why not just spend your energy observing yourself, and getting rid of the junk you don't need? Forget all the comparisons!

16.
In your book you describe The Energy Thief. I never realized that people actually rob us of energy. How come I never saw it that way?

We were never told about that. We thought that things happen the way they happen and that's how it's supposed to be. But when you understand the need for keeping your energy, you become an "Energy Conservationist." Your energy becomes very valuable to you, and you don't want people stealing it from you. You can only have insight into life by having tremendous energy for it. So, be an "Energy Conservationist."

17.

Do all twenty difficult people in your book have one thing in common: vanity?

Yes. Difficult people never consider other people. They are always wrongly self-involved. That's one of the reasons they're so difficult. All they ever think about is what they want. They're always bumping into other people psychologically and causing problems. We don't want to be that kind of person. That's why the book was written. We've all been that way, and we don't want to be that way anymore.

18.

Have I been wasting my time all these years trying to figure out why my mother-in-law is the way she is—always criticizing me—when I should have been trying to figure out why it bothers me so much?

My dear lady, the reason she criticizes you is because you didn't marry her son sooner! She'd been trying to get rid of him for years! After living with him for awhile, can't you see why she wanted to lose him earlier? Seriously, the thing is that we have an inner criticizer who won't leave us alone. And because we listen to that voice inside us, we also listen to the person outside. We have to see clearly that this is the case. When we do see it fully, both criticizers will cease to have any effect on us. Who we really are has no connection with either one.

19.

How come I don't see difficult people coming until it's too late?

We are seldom really aware of where we are and what we are doing. We must keep our mind where our body is and not let it wander off into the past or the future. We need to know what is going on, moment to moment, inside and outside of us. Catch yourself drifting off into a pleasant or unpleasant daydream, and bring yourself back.

Be intensely aware. It will solve lots of problems with difficult people just to know where you are and what you are doing. At the same time know what you're thinking and feeling—what's happening inside you. You can't do anything well if you are somewhere else psychologically. In fact, if difficult people could really see themselves in action, they wouldn't be that way.

20.
You say difficult people are really only children in disguise. Why is it so hard to see that and not react negatively?

The fact is we really know very little about practical human psychology. The reason we have problems with people who have grown-up bodies but still have a childish psychology, is because we don't understand *ourselves*. The key is self-understanding. We then can see other people the way they really are, because we see ourselves the way we really are. Sit with yourself for fifteen minutes every morning with a light spirit. Just watch your thoughts. Let them come, and let them go. You can learn a lot doing this.

21.
Why is it that a certain person—really a classic example of The Demander—annoys me so much, but doesn't seem to annoy other people?

I can tell you from personal experience, that whenever there was somebody who really agitated me, really bothered me, whom I really didn't like, it was because they were just like me! By being judgmental toward them, I hid that truth from myself. So what a person can do—and I recommend this to everybody—is to spend more time with people who really upset them so that you can see what the problem really is. You will see it has to do with the *image* you have of the kind of person you are as opposed to the kind of person you *really* are. To see the truth about yourself is tremendously freeing. It's a terrible load to pretend to be something or someone you're not.

22.

Where I work there's a good example of The Energy Thief. He steals a lot of energy from me and everybody else by not doing what he says he will do. Is there a trick to getting people to do what they promise they'll do?

If you find the trick, let me know! It's a fact, though, that it's very unusual these days to find people who will follow through on what they say they're going to do. And, what usually happens when they don't do it? We don't bring it up—because of our image. We want them to like us. Or, we get angry and negative. Those are the two ways we usually respond. Neither is the correct way to handle a difficult situation like that. The correct way to handle it is: *Don't* do any of the things that are *incorrect*. That's the correct way of handling it. For instance, don't act out your negativity. Just consciously bear your own negativity, burn in your own negative reactions we could say, so you'll give it up. Give up the hostility. And, don't placate the other individual. Now, do you know what to do?

23.

When I first met my husband, he was so charming and sweet. We laughed a lot and he couldn't do enough for me. Now, he's dull and boring and grouchy most of the time. How can a man change so drastically!

Look! The man you married was a dream man; now he's more of a nightmare. But here's a different question: Can a beautiful dove turn into an ugly crow? If a person is a particular way, they are that way all the time—they're just not showing it. The problem is: when we want something from somebody, we see the obvious, but we ignore it! There is always a very quiet voice inside that points out things to us we should consider, but when we are driven by desire we refuse to heed the warning. We won't acknowledge to ourselves how that person really is. When we want something from each other, we're both on our best behavior. So you have these two people, two crows, pretending to be doves! Then later both realize they got mixed up with a crow. We have to be forthright from the beginning—eyes wide open.

24.

Shouldn't we be honest and direct with difficult people instead of trying to be diplomatic and not ruffle their feathers?

It depends. Sometimes it's right to be tactful. You don't want to be tactless. Oftentimes a person is upset or irritated because of something that happened, some problem or event or person they don't know how to handle. They're being difficult because they are upset or negative over whatever it was. Maybe the right thing to do now is to be very tactful with them and handle them gently because they are easily set off. And what's the point of making it worse? There's a law of physics that says that for every action there is a reaction. They'll take it that you're pushing them, and they'll push back, thinking they're defending themselves. And what about "Judge not lest ye be judged"?

25.

When I leave a bad situation with a difficult person, I carry negative feelings with me. Why can't I just drop it?

Here's what none of us want to hear. It's much, much better to stay on the battleground. That is, stay in the middle of the situation you don't know how to handle. Eventually the situation itself will teach you how to handle it. You're going to have to take some bumps, some psychological hits. But if you stay there long enough, it will become so uncomfortable that you'll understand what's going on. By staying uncomfortable you can discover and dispel the real source of the discomfort. The answer is always inside. The problem is inside, and the solution is inside. I must use the situation to discover that healing fact.

26.

Murray, one thing I've seen from working with the ideas in the handbook is how much I love being weak, instead of inwardly standing up and reaching for a higher way to handle difficult people— such as turning the other cheek. How can I stop being what I always am? I want to be strong and compassionate.

Correct handling of difficult people is really self-discovery—learning things about ourselves that we don't want to know. By learning that I don't deal with people properly, I am gaining understanding. But I must not beat myself up over what I see. I must be indifferent toward it; I must just observe it. I don't have to do anything. If I stay out of it and just observe it, the time will come when I won't do it anymore, because my Essence isn't that way. It will be a natural change. Because I've allowed the light to come into a dark room and illuminate it.

27.

Why do I replay an encounter with a difficult person over and over in my mind?

It's the broken record syndrome. All of us have had that experience. Isn't the reason I do it because I want to convince myself that I'm right and they're wrong? And of course, the other person thinks that I'm just as difficult as I think they are. So I just keep running it over in my mind, maybe changing it each time a little bit so I am never the bad person; I'm always the good person. Isn't this pure egotism?

28.

The book seems to say that everyone is just like me, cooped up inside his or her own psychology, and that we need to look inside ourselves first. Is that right?

Right. I'm in my little world, and they're in their little world. What we're having really is a clash of worlds. There's not really the interaction we think there is—no real relationship. The only way there can be a real relationship, is when I lay down my sword. When I quit being so Touchy Touchy, quit saying that everybody is doing this to me, and all that sort of stuff. We have to lay down the sword—all the hostility, resentment, envy, and so on. It isn't easy, because it's so familiar. We're so used to it. We feel that it's important and that it keeps us safe. But it doesn't. It's always a double-edged sword. Whatever I do to another person I must first do to myself. It's always that way under law. I cannot hurt another human being without hurting myself first. It's law. Spiritual law.

29.

How do I keep in mind all the right responses to difficult people that you suggest in your book?

Look! If you fill your mind with all these ideas and try to remember them, then your mind will be cluttered with all that. You don't want to have a cluttered mind. You want to have a relaxed, open, easy-flowing mind. So what you need to do is to feel the rightness of what is said either in a book or in a class. Just do that, and then, on its own, it will come to you at the right time. Don't fill your mind with all these ideas. For one thing it will make you rigid. Then you'll get in fights over it. Don't we always get into trouble with other people because we have all these fixed ideas about what's right and wrong? Bend in the breeze. Be flexible. You need to see certain things and feel the rightness of them, and that will bring about a change in you.

You need to keep the essence of this book in your heart! I'm not trying to teach people something I wrote. This is about people reading these ideas, and then applying them to themselves by looking at their own lives. And then saying that Murray is right, or he is wrong, or I don't know. If it is right, it is right all by itself and doesn't need anything else. Then anybody can use it and feel the rightness of it.

30.

I love the way the book refers to spiritual ways, such as to turn the other cheek. I know that's the right way to act, but when I'm in certain situations with other people, I forget all about that and I just react. How can I stop my wrong reactions?

I understand. What you're saying is that you are swept away before you know what happened. Even though you can feel the wrongness of it, or the rightness of not doing it, you're still swept away by it. The key is: slow down physically. The whole world is against that—you have to go against the whole world to do it. But slow down physically. And if you'll slow down physically, you will slow down your thoughts and your emotions. Then you'll be able to catch yourself before you say or do what you would have said or done. It will become a conscious act, instead of an unconscious, mechanical, negative reaction.

31.

Not to react to difficult people, for instance, not to express your annoyance—wouldn't some say you're a hypocrite or dishonest?

Generally speaking you are better off tending to your own knitting and not being critical toward other people or trying to straighten them out. In my life I found I was much better off not doing that. First of all, I was never able to change anyone. Nor have I seen anybody else do it. So I'm a lot better off changing me. I *can* do that. And probably a lot of people would appreciate it!

32.

The other day someone tried to bait me into an argument. And because of your book I knew I didn't have to answer. It was good to see what was going on and just watch my reactions without getting into it.

Right. And that's what we all need to do more. Just to *not do* what we always do with regard to difficult people. So then we can have the new experience of seeing things about ourselves that we never knew were there. That's really exciting.

I mean that's real life! Instead of the boring, humdrum life most people have, constantly trying to prove that I'm right and you're wrong and all that. There's nothing nicer than trying to prove you're wrong to yourself! And then join forces with the other people!

33.

In the book, you say that Difficult Person Number Twenty is me. Recently I saw that in my work, I set up an unrealistic, impossible schedule in my mind and then anxiously tried to fulfill that schedule. Is that what you mean?

Yes. Do you know why you do it? Number one it makes you feel very important, to be on this mission impossible. Plus, it makes you feel superior. Because all these other people, all these underlings, don't have this mission. I'm so great; I have lots of stuff to do. And third, you can vibrate. You can feel really anxious over it and make yourself really sick. Believe it or not people like all three of those things.

34.

Isn't part of the problem that our society trains us and expects us to become difficult people, since it instills in us all kinds of wrong attitudes and behavior?

Society doesn't understand itself, so all it can possibly do is to give the children of society the same lack of understanding. That's where we pick it up. But that doesn't mean we have to stay that way. We can self-educate.

35.

Something goes wrong in my relations with someone, and I always get my feelings hurt. This is a wrong reaction isn't it?

All of us have had our feelings hurt. The best thing I can say is that we all need to grow up. All of us, no matter what our age is, need to get over it and grow up.

This is another instance of not understanding our own psychology and how our mind works. It's really nothing but thoughts—thinking about one person or another. But I think it's me thinking the thoughts. No. It's just the thought process mechanically operating. But I'm the one that suffers. It's nothing but thought. And that's why it's so good to be around difficult people and get knocked around enough to get knocked loose from all of the wrong ideas I've been holding onto for so long. Then I can really understand my own psychology and understand others' as well. It all has to come from within. No matter where you go or what books you read—ultimately, it all has to come from within. You have to be a TD—a Truth Detective!

36.

So the competent person or the insecure person I think I am...those are just thoughts, right?

Just imagine. If I didn't label myself and I didn't want to be somebody, wouldn't that eliminate a lot of difficult people in my life? People are difficult because I want them to look at me and treat me in a certain way. What if I didn't have any ideas about that— that I'm this marvelous person who should always be treated in a special way? Maybe people have been treating me the way they do because of the way I am.

37.

Shouldn't we start looking at difficult people and awkward situations differently—as opportunities—instead of something to avoid or oppose?

Absolutely. It's inner-development school, that's what it is. Every situation, every difficult person is a teacher that is going to show us what we need to learn about ourselves. That's the only way to be free of a person or situation—to be free of what I don't understand about myself. When I understand myself, it smooths everything out and that's it!

38.

When someone challenges my ideas about myself, I get upset and call them a difficult person. Why do I let their behavior dictate how I feel?

What if we went about life this way: "Look! Obviously there's so much about life that I don't know or understand. So what I'm going to do is to spend my whole life learning. Teaching myself about life and what is true according to higher understanding and higher psychology." I can never reach the top of that high mountain; therefore, I can never be the master and never be the greatest because this kind of learning is infinite.

We need to have that kind of right attitude; that is, we have to assume responsibility for what goes on inwardly. I am a student of life. I want to learn more about life. I do it by observing myself as I live life. If we all keep doing what we are doing now, then we keep getting what we get. The only way to get anything better is when we don't do what we've always done that makes it worse! If I eat certain foods that make me feel bad, I will continue to feel bad. If I stop eating those foods, I will stop feeling bad. It's the same thing psychologically. I don't know how I will feel if I stop doing the things I always do. But I know I won't feel the way I was feeling. Which is good news. Plus, I'm talking about a way of living your life where you really can't make any mistakes if your heart is right. Every time you make a mistake, it's a lesson.

39.

Most of the difficult people in my life are in the past—my memories of what difficult people have done or said at sometime or another. How does one handle this situation?

Find the nearest trash can, put all of that trash in it, and be through with it forever. Just know that unpleasant, negative memories are bad for you. It would be no different if you go to the doctor and told him you weren't feeling well. He'll tell you you're eating too many candy bars and drinking too many soft drinks and that they are messing up your system. So what you should do is to lay off that stuff and not have anything to do with it. It's making you sick. I'm saying the same thing to you. All of that stuff is making you sick. Don't have anything to do with it. And, on top of that, the way you remember it, probably isn't really the way it happened anyway. It's all over and done with. It doesn't exist anymore, except in your memory. That's the only place the painful memories exist. In reality those events don't exist anymore. You can realize that by psychologically throwing the bad memories in the trash. Be through with them. When one comes up again and wants you to replay the whole business again in your mind, say, "No, I'm not doing that anymore!" and have nothing to do with it. If it comes up 150 times, still just say, "No, I'll have nothing to do with you!" It'll get the idea eventually and vanish.

40.

Is your book reaching a lot of people? It's clear there's a lot of need for help in dealing with difficult people.

There's nothing nicer than telling people about right things, but at the same time, not proselytizing. They either want it or they don't, and that's it. That's the way I live my life. I'm not trying to sell anybody on anything. They either want to hear more or they don't. Let's all want more!

Bright Candles to Light the Way: Something Extra for Readers of This Handbook

1. Carrying a grudge weighs you down. Let your spirit soar!

2. Welcome life's challenges for if we are teachable each contains an amazing lesson.

3. Never ask a donkey how to fly.

4. Letting others think for you dulls the mind. Thinking for yourself brightens the spirit.

5. Won't you agree that being good should come before doing good?

6. Working to discover who you really are is the only thing worth doing. Why? Because it is the meaning of life.

7. Blaming others for our problems is an attempt to hide from them, but they always find us.

8. Everything in life costs something. Want to be authentically cheerful? Give up your love of sadness.

9. The three L's: Learn Truth. Love Truth. Live Truth.

10. Cosmic fact: If you know where you're going it'll be boring when you get there.

11. Life is really fun when you decide to climb to the mountain top and not take yourself along.

12. True lasting pleasure does exist, but not where most people look. Now you know where to find it.

About the Author

Murray Oxman is a bestselling author, seminar leader, and psychological researcher. He has been featured on radio and TV shows and in newspapers throughout the country. He's published in the prestigious *American Journal of Psychology*. In over twenty years Murray has led thousands of classes and seminars.

He emphatically says he is not telling anyone what to do, either in his writings or talks. He is only saying what he has learned the hard way, by self-observation and being ruthlessly honest with himself. Murray lives and teaches classes in Corvallis, Oregon.

To contact Murray Oxman or for information about classes in Corvallis, Oregon, please write or call:

Success Without Stress
5445 NW Crescent Valley Dr
Corvallis, Oregon 97330
541.752.0870